THE MYTH
OF THE
ABSENTEE FATHER

(A Transcript of Events)

by

Marcos R. Wise

DORRANCE
PUBLISHING CO
EST. 1920
PITTSBURGH, PENNSYLVANIA 15238

Dorrance Publishing Co
585 Alpha Drive
Pittsburgh, PA 15238
Visit our website at www.dorrancebookstore.com

ISBN: 978-1-4809-4878-5
eISBN: 978-1-4809-4901-0

PRELUDE

I feel that an individual that views themselves as a good person should never stand by when unfairness and wronging is done to another person regardless of the perpetrator's status. If you do then you are no better than that perpetrator.

I can deal with anything in this world with the exception of a "Blatant Liar". And what I mean by a blatant liar is an individual that is not facing any immediate physical danger, incarceration in a Penal Colony (Prison and/or Jail), destroying an innocent person's peace ultimately, and most of all not allowing an individual proper communication when it is needed. And of course giving false statements when there is no reason or rhyme for it.

I can deal with any person that does not possess these characteristics.

Most importantly, any person that believes and draw an ultimate conclusion without all of the facts and doing the homework on their own, is nothing more than a Fool. There are always other factors to a scenario.

And this is mines concerning the Myth that there no good fathers in the community.

This is not a long book but at least one that gives immediate substance and communication to the reader. I also came to the realization that this is also, hopefully, an indirect letter to my Children, especially my Daughter who is truly an innocent victim. She loves her siblings (brother & sister) very much. And I want for her to know that her tribulations are no fault of your own. I hope this gives you some understanding of why you may feel that I let you down.

I wanted to make sure in the process of writing this book that I was not bias but objective in any and all facts that I encountered while establishing my mindset for an ultimate opinion. So let me start by giving you a little background information on myself. I was raised in a two parent household in Tuskegee, Alabama with 4 siblings. I was the 4th child with 2 older sisters and 1 older brother. I have a younger sister. My Father was the bread winner and my Mother was a traditional housewife. I figured growing up that this was the way Americans strived for in a nuclear family layout. But at 41 years old I can finally and wholeheartedly say that is not the case. When growing up I was inundated with the appearance and assumption that there were little or no fathers willing to step up to the plate. But sadly after life experiences with two Women that I produced children with and speaking with many fathers since, I have reached the conclusion that it's a Myth about the absentee Father. In fact the culprit is the Mother; sadly to say. Before you become emotional about this statement I ask that you objectively hear me out; in other words turn off what you "think" your brain should hear and accept what it "needs" to hear. Rather you ultimately agree with me or not, hear me out. Although this problem is common in all nationalities, I will be partly speaking from a perspective of Color and Race.

My mindset development because I feel at times it is Black women with this mentality. I don't know but a lot of objective information has pointed that way in my opinion. But with a logical mind we are sometimes forced to think objectively.

I will start at the ending briefly which bought me this conclusion. It involved a major court case with the Arkansas Department of Human Services in which I attempted to retrieve my Daughter M from their custody. I was not responsible for her entering their custody at any rate. This was a heart wrenching two Year Battle which I am convinced that the court had no intention in acting on Objective lawful issues but on pure biases. After Judge B terminated my Parental Rights because of missed visits and my so-called attitude with my Daughter's unskilled counselor. I remind you that none of my actions were the reason my Daughter was taken into the Department of Human Services Custody but because of the Mother. Til this day it still seems surreal to me and this was a Black Judge executing this. Judge W B of the Division in the Circuit Court of Pulaski County, Arkansas. As a matter of fact I won three contempt charges against the Mother in attempting to remove her prior to this situation to my home for safety. These and other pertinent facts were purposely ignored in my opinion to help perpetuate the mindset of unfit Black Fathers.

Or, "Am I Wrong?" I'll let you decide.

Starting with the "Love of My Life", Y L S from Chicago, Illinois. Mannnn!!! What a beautiful woman. The sex, body, the whole nine yards. Or was I right or wrong? I meet Y in a grocery store back in late 1997 called at the time Jitney Jungle on West Markham in Little Rock,

Arkansas. Let me remind you that I was 27 years old with no children yearning to have what my Father had, and she was 25 years old with 2 children. A boy (J) who was 4 and a beautiful young girl (D) who was 3 months old. I instantly fell in love with little D because it gave me the chance to start my exercise for being a Father one day; preferably with this woman which happen two years later.

My first born by this woman, who I was thankful for the opportunity to be a Beginning Father to her first two children, was J D W. When it's all said and done this woman gave me the most beautiful thing in this world which was the potential family I always wanted; in her children J and D but also the Son J that she bore for me in the year 2000. I was so prepared to continue to be a Good Father in thinking that when it was all said and done the Child(ren) would come first. No matter what mindset we encountered that it would be about that. Well four years later in 2003 began my journey in realizing a much, much different road to be a Father in America. Being a father of color in America. Well many disturbances and arguing with the law later, Y finally married in the wedding dress I bought her to another man 6 months after our final parting. As much as I felt my pride hurt I still appreciated the most beautiful gift she gave me; My Son.

Now I want to make clear this is not a book attempting to place the blame or discuss where our hearts(mindsets) or other connotations that could be used to describe our relationship; but a focus on society's view and help in a society for Fathers in our community.

After our separation I made sure to stay in my boy's life as much as possible; even wanting to stay in his siblings life that I was a part of for a beautiful 4 ½ years. But from when he was barely able to walk to present it seems at least to me that this woman made the most outrageous obstacles for me to do this. And it still continues. I turned to the judicial system to aid with my plight and it did not help. Was it because the Judge that presided over this case for 10 years was a, "Black Woman"?

Ten Years I remind you. I finally had enough from Judge W August of 2012 when she refused to give me more time with my Son; Citing that she won't because we were not still getting alone. "How Is That My Fought?" Instead of looking out for what was fair the only way that this Judge was to give me my just do was to jump through the Mother's hoops. Thus making the Judge in this case, not a neutral party but a cheerleader. I realized at that point I needed to transfer my case out of that court immediately.

To regress for a quick point, during the course of this relationship I made sure to never "bad mouthed", the other two kids fathers in that I found it very disrespectful. As a matter of fact I wanted them to have a healthy relationship with their fathers. At times the mother would spit out negative things about them and I immediately stopped her. I feel that no Man or (Woman) should go out their way to hinder a relationship between a Child and their Father. And it is really pitiful when a male does this. The type of male that is so insecure that they will interfere and cause confusion with their mate because of their past relationship(s). And what is so sad many women are quickly to pick these type of men because of their own insecurities. In other words being biologically a male but have all the characteristics of a menstruating female. This was one of the barriers dealing with my son for pickups and drop offs. This man was easily manipulated by YS because of weak mindedness. I remind you that I had no romantic or sexual attraction to his mate anymore. I just wanted my Son's time. And do I need to really tell you the catalyst for it? I can honestly say that I made every attempt to respect this man and wanted dearly to respect him as a step-parent but it was literally impossible because of his issues. I wanted to be cordial because this man resided with my son. Regardless of the source of those issues he had I didn't care anymore. The ultimate issue for me was and is my son. I can only speculate that if that behavior was directed towards me, than how he was verbally representing me to my son; my hands were tied because the court will not perform their duties. Quite frankly this court has blatantly shown me that they do not care. The only solace is that my son will soon be eighteen and hopefully hindsight will allow him to view this situation in its entirety. But I knew the one aspect that I could control was my behavior. In that for the most part I made certain to conduct myself with respect in his presence and making sure not to exacerbate his stress.

We all have insecurities at one time or another, but there is absolutely no reason for a man to be jealous of another man. For what? A woman is going do what she wants to do, how she wants to and when she wants to. If a man is doing what he is suppose to in making his life complete there is no time for jealously. Like Jay-Z said, "Males shouldn't be jealous, that's a female trait." These are the things I had to deal with because the courts just could not bring themselves to adjudicate the case properly dealing with my custody and visitation issues.

Before I begin into what some may call a rant I want to give you some brief layperson statistics. On a yearly average of the Black Children born, above 70 percent of them are to unwed Black Mothers. Not that there is anything wrong in my opinion in abstaining from marriage of course. I have never been married mostly because of choice. But I want to start with a baseline here. Let's keep going.

According to the Minority Families and Child Support: Data Analysis done in the beginning of the 21st Century, the proportion of African-American Mothers with legal agreements with Child Support Enforcement were from 31 percent in 1990 to 47 percent by 2002. Starting for the first time in 2002, the percent of Black custodial Mothers who had a child support order outnumbered those that did not. Do you mean to tell me that there are so many Black fathers that deserves this or is it just a trend that women think is "cute". I'm pretty sure that these Dads would have no problem taking care and being in their child(ren) lives. But who wants to go through unnecessary Drama caused by the Custodial parent to do so.

According to a rolling out politics website, an article and study done by Terry Shropshire April 2011 concluded that more than 59 percent of black women who have more than one child have different men that created them. Hispanics were a far distant at 35 percent, and white women at 22 percent. There is something massively wrong with that gap. Once again whether you want to or not you must see how this mindset toward Black Fathers from Black Women is no good for the raising and proper upbringing of a child. Not for America period.

Every time I ventured to the Child Support Enforcement Office I personally observed at-least a 4 to 1 ratio of Black women to White women that were there to file cases. And I promise you that although I am quoting my own observations; my numbers quoted are on a conservative end. In other words there were many times where that ratio was much more in favor of Black women but I would like to err on the side of caution. With those statistics let us remember that the Black population in the United States is between 13 – 15 percent. Which make these numbers even more disturbing.

I'm going out on a limb here in thinking that the established system really doesn't want Black family units and is using the Women of Color to induce this ideology. And what's so sad is that they are falling for this foolishness hook, line, and sinker. Ignoring the fact that these children will be our caretakers in the future. But I wonder why????

Now back to my first scenario I was discussing earlier involving my Son. This case was heard for 10 years by Judge W, a Black Woman. During this decade she did not once grant anything in my favor; not even the most conservative request. And by the way the turnover employment rate for court staff in this office was extremely high. Every time I had a hearing there were different entities in the staff. My issue was visitation.

One of the basics for her refusing to grant my modification requests was that in her own words were, "Because ya'll are not getting alone." That wasn't my fought. The reason I was requesting changes was because of the Mother's behavior. And if the Mother was being fair and we were getting alone than what was the use for the Judge in the first place? So ridiculous!

After my anguish maxed from this Judge I finally requested a transfer of my file to another court in which she denied. After going back and forth through unnecessary red tape with this Woman (Judge) I decided to file a complaint with the Arkansas Judicial Disciplinary Commission showing her biasness against me directly and indirectly. Finally my case was granted for reassignment in the Pulaski County, Arkansas Circuit Court.

Even though it was transferred I faced the same obstacles after reassignment of the case. I was at times thinking, "was my case actually "randomly" reassigned or "placed?" I have no proof of either scenario so once again I prefer to err on the side of caution. But this I know for sure, even with this different Judge it was a continuation of the same biasness. I don't want to appear that I think all Judges are this way. As a matter of fact one of the most intellectual and impartial Judges I ever met was in my Daughter's case, Judge V S, before the Department of Human Services involvement. Even when something did not go in my favor I was still left with the comfort of impartiality. And that is a characteristic that I find very positive in an authoritative figure. Till this day I have a great and deep respect for Judge V S. This bought me to the next life changing view on this system in the United States.

Now let's jump to my equally most preciously joy which is my Daughter M that was born 4 years later by a different woman. I'm not going into intricate detail on this matter because it would be too long. Therefore I will cut to the meat and potatoes of the matter.

Beginning since my Daughter M was born I had to file 3 contempt motions in the Pulaski County Circuit Court in which the Mother was hindering my visitation. In two of these three she was found guilty with the last one resulting in her spending a day in jail. This mother also filed 4 Orders of Protection against me in which all were dismissed and her also being fined Monterrey for the court's time being wasted on one of them. Judge V S was completely fair in that he viewed the situation through objective (right or wrong) lenses. He was White. I mention these individuals ethnicity because I want you as the reader to have all of the objective facts in that you can draw your own conclusion. In my objective mindset, I feel that if it quacks like a duck and walks like a duck, than it's probably a duck. In other words what's the probability that it was a coincident that my most unfair decisions dealing with my cases involving my Children came from non white entities. You Decide.

The one person that truly understood my plight with my Daughter M was my appellant attorney L.L. She wrote the most beautiful brief to the Arkansas Court of Appeals. The next statement is L.L.'s quote from that brief in the Statement of Facts which summarize everything on my part; here it is:

> **"In an order filed September 12, 2013, the Pulaski County Circuit Court terminated Marcos Wise"s parental rights to his eight year old daughter, M.W. Mr. Wise appeals from the termination order.**
>
> **M.W.'s removal was from her mother, with whom Mr. Wise did not reside. He was the non-custodial father, and enjoyed visitation pursuant to a court order. Although Mr. Wise was not responsible for M.W.'s removal, M.W. was never placed in his custody because the court ordered reunification with the mother.**
>
> **Mr. Wise became frustrated with the situation, and began to lash out at DHS staff and M.W.'s ther-**

apist, who recommended reunification with the mother. Although the court ordered him to complete anger management because of this, with which Mr. Wise complied and benefited from, the court believe Mr. Wise to be foolish and unstable. As a result, the court terminated his parental rights.

Mr. Wise filed a timely notice of appeal from that order and this brief follows."

These documents can easily be verified through the Pulaski County, Arkansas Circuit Court Clerk records.

This case involved one Mother and 3 Fathers, all of whom had their parental rights terminated to their respective children. That same layout of fraternal prodigies is with my Son's Mother except my Daughter was the Mother's first born and my Son was his Mother's third born. However I was the only Father in my Daughter's case who fought through the initial court system and the appeal process. Beginning to end.

Not to give an excuse for any absentee parent but I understand more fully at this stage of my life why some Fathers excuse themselves. If I knew all the crap I had to go through just to love my children I probably would have given up also. Now when a woman tells me her story about their kid's father not being around, I kind of have a "raised eyebrow" thought towards her words. Untrusted.

Now to my Son for a sec.

After many callings with the police to obtain my Son I decided to go back to Court after one year of Having the first Judge (Black Woman) recused. After ten years Judge W of the Circuit Court Juvenile Division would not check the Mother just one time? Really? Hear we go with another Judge and low and behold everything became fair again. Or so I thought. "Is it a coincidence that this Judge who was White more [FAIR]?; I'm just saying.

9

Although my Son's mother continues to make wild allegations to keep confusion up it is a matter of time till it has to stop legally. What was so exhausting was that she fed off of my Daughter's case to give her lies more momentum. The thing that kept me sane during this process was internally laughing at some officials that were falling for it. No disrespect to those officials (Judges) but if I did not internally laugh at the weak mindedness of them than I would not have been able to survive emotionally. My Daughter's counselor made a blanketed statement to me stating she feels that I could have done more. When I pressed her on how besides going in and physically and unlawfully removing her without a Court Order. She had no answer. But just like society she was drawing conclusions that had no merit. Just saying something for sake of saying it. The proper information was right before her to conclude that the mother was at fought but she along with some Judges are just too weak to objectively judge a woman. I want to reiterate the word SOME (Not All) in this statement. Why? I cannot come up with one rational idea. The only time when some of these individuals become objective is when a catastrophe happens or worst. It is dumbfounding for me to observe an authoritative figure incapable of objectively. If it wasn't so cynical and personally damaging it would be really funny.

But I had to continue to focus on my Daughter which was a more pressing issue. I finally had help from my Appellant Attorney L.L. Thank God.

This is the exact argument literally that my appellant attorney L.L. wrote which is way more than I could have:

Statement of Case:
"In an order filed September 12, 2013, the Pulaski County Circuit Court terminated Marcos Wise's parental rights to his eight-year old daughter, M.W.

M.W.'s removal was from the mother, with whom Mr. Wise did not reside. He was the non-custodial father, and enjoyed visitation pursuant to a court order from another court. Although Mr. Wise was not responsible for M.W's removal, M.W. Was never placed in his custody because the court ordered reunification with the mother.

Mr. Wise became frustrated with the situation, and began to lash out at DHS staff and M.W.'s therapist, who recommended reunification with the mother. Although the court ordered him to complete anger management because of this, with which Mr. Wise complied and benefited from, the court believed Mr. Wise to be foolish and unstable. As a result, the court terminated his parental rights.

Mr. Wise filed a timely notice of appeal from that order, and this brief follows.

Wow, some one that believed in me. I did not care that she was a white woman as long it would help me save my baby. Now next is the argument she made:

M.W., born ????, was taken into custody with her younger brothers on February 22, 2012, pursuant to an emergency petition filed by DHS. M.W. was residing with her mother at the time of her removal, although Marcos Wise enjoyed court-ordered visitation with M.W. This is significant, because Mr. Wise was in no way responsible for M.W's removal, as demonstrated by the affidavit attached to the Petition for Emergency Custody, the trial court's specific findings in the Order for Emergency Custody that the mother was the cause of the children's removal, and the Probable Cause Order in which the court found that emergency conditions existed which necessitated removal of the children "from the custody of the mother."

Despite Mr. Wise's lack of involvement in the circumstances necessitating the removal of M.W., and having done nothing to demonstrate that he was anything other than the fit non-custodial parent that a prior court had already deemed him to be, the juvenile court stripped him of presumption of fitness and ordered him to have supervised visits with M.W., required him to submit to a psychological evaluation and drug and alcohol screens, and to submit to a home study. Three months after M.W. Was removed, she was adjudicated dependent-neglected. The Adjudication Order referenced only the mother in regard to the reasons M.W. was dependent-neglected, but the court continued to disregard Mr. Wise as a fit parent for placement of M.W., saying only that "Mr. Wise deserves a serious look regarding M.W.," and that he "can work with ADHS to see if he can be a suitable placement for M.W." Mr. Wise had already attended every hearing, submitted to a DNA test proving he was M.W.'s father, and had already begun psychological testing with Dr. Paul DeYoub.

On May 22, 2012, Dr. DeYoub completed a report in which he did not give Mr. Wise a diagnosis. He concluded that Mr. Wise was capable of caring

> for M.W., although Dr. DeYoub recommended that Mr. Wise complete parenting classes since M.W. had some behavioral issues.

I want to briefly interject that working with DHS was as frustrating and trifling as working with the worst of the worst individuals ever. Was it a coincidence that 100 percent of my dealings were with black women in this Organization? I'm just saying. Also my Daughter had behavioral issues because of the Mother's environment, not mine. Duh! But back to the literal argument of my appellant Attorney.

> Other than parenting classes, Dr. DeYoub recommended only that DHS verify the history that Mr. Wise self-reported, which was that he had a Bachelor's degree and was about to complete his Master's in Rehabilitation Counseling.
>
> On July 24, 2012, the trail court held a Permanency Planning hearing and entered an order finding that Mr. Wise had made an "effort to comply." The court noted that Mr. Wise needed to "visit more frequently and possibly be included in family therapy with M.W."- a service that should have been offered long before the passage of five months if the court was going to make Mr. Wise participate in services- and even opened the option for other relatives to take placement of the child despite, again, Mr, Wise having done nothing to precipitate such an attitude of exclusion toward him.
>
> The following day, due to Mr. Wise's understandable exasperation and frustration, Mr. Wise (acting *pro se* because the court had not appointed

him an attorney) filed an Emergency Request for Hearing and Motion to Release Juvenile Child into Father's Custody. In his motion, he stated that the caseworker, J.D. "falsely" testified in court at the previously day's permanency planning hearing that Mr. Wise was "resistant to DHS requests" and that it was J.D. who told Mr. Wise to "stop calling and emailing so much because it gets on my nerves"- that "when we need you, we will contact you." Mr. Wise further stated in the motion that he believed J.D. did not care about his position on anything related to M.W., despite passing a home study and submitting to alcohol and drug screens, and proving he had a college education, as reported to Dr. DeYoub. Mr. Wise attached a previous email he had written to J.D. expressing these same sentiments, thus demonstrating that he had not been passive, but merely frustrated and "very emotionally exhausted" due to the poor treatment of him by DHS...........

And of course J.D. is a Black Woman.

I want to make a quick point that within a six month period my friend and next door neighbor passed, my Daughter was taken into DHS, I completed my Master's Program and had major surgery on both my feet. Once again no one cared but continued to give the Mother every benefit of the doubt that almost had a catastrophic ending for my Daughter. These people had their mind made that they would rather see the demise of my child than to acknowledge that she had a Father in her life ready to step up. But in my opinion they wanted to keep up the facade of the Absentee Black Father. And I remind you that these were other Black Women doing this! But Let me continue with my attorney's words.

> DHS and M.W.'s mother responded to Mr. Wise's motion asking that it be denied. Mr. Wise then filed another *pro se* pleading – a Request for Production of Documents, stating that while he was not an attorney, he was an important stake-holder in the case, and entitled to any information provided by DHS to M.W.'s mother. The Depart-ment summarily dismissed him.
>
> Mr. Wise then filed another *pro se* motion to release M.W. into his custody, stating that he had remedied the issues of sporadic visitation that con-cerned the trail court in the August 2, 2012, Per-manency Planning Order. Mr. Wise laid out his issues with the visitation schedule, saying that he had a job, that DHS would cancel visits and staffings after he had informed his employer that he would be needing time off for those events, and when Mr. Wise would express his frustration about the cancellations, the Department would state that the event would be made up, which caused prob-lems for Mr. Wise, as he said, he did not have "the luxury of altering my work schedule at any given time and it is very unfair to be asked to do so." He then asked a rather apposite question, "What is an individual to do when the reason his child is not released to him is because of a lack of visits and at the same time he can't [visit] because of DHS?" Mr. Wise's growing frustration was evident in his

Motion when he explained that he had made every endeavor to meet the court's requirements by keeping in touch with DHS through calls and emails, filing pleadings, and taking off work for visits and other tasks, including a psychological evaluation, a home study, drug screens, alcohol tests, and more. Mr. Wise asked simply what more he had to do to stop being punished for the actions of M.W.'s mother.

The record demonstrates that the Department cancelled staffings, did not return emails to Mr. Wise, and cancelled visits that had to be made up. The Attorney *Ad Litem* filed a response stating that while Mr. Wise had been visiting regularly with M.W., he had not stated a basis for the granting of custody to him, and that he bore some responsibility for the delay "in all of this because he was not visiting regularly until August 2012." The court entered an order on September 28, 2012, denying Mr. Wise's motion, stating that his compliance with court orders was not the determining factor, and that placing custody with him would be "premature". The court scheduled the case for another permanency planning hearing on December 11, 2012, to "determine the parental fitness of the parents and whether a placement is in the child's best interest."

Trust me that the only thing on my mind at this point was, "REALLY!!!"

After the December hearing, the court entered an order finding that while it was "clear to the Court

> that Mr. Wise ha[d] made gains" and that the
> "Court want[ed] him to continue to make gains,"
> the goal of the case "shall continue to be reunifica-
> tion with the mother." The court expanded Mr.
> Wise's visits with M.W., but made it clear that the
> court would work toward transitioning M.W. Into
> her mother's custody. Mr. Wise had to undergo
> four additional supervised visits, however, before
> he would be allowed to have any unsupervised visits
> – all to be followed up by M.W.'s therapist, B.W.

Talking about a superficial woman B.W. was; man! During my visits she and the caseworker would gossip about their personal lives as if they were in the "HOOD." But lets continue with the attorney's words.

> This point in the case became pivotal. It was at this
> point that Mr. Wise had been pushed to his limit,
> and rightfully so, and he began to lash out at Ther-
> apists B.W. and DHS staff. He began to send a mul-
> titude of text messages to Therapist W with
> complaints about her court testimony and her
> counseling skills (presumably because she had rec-
> ommended that M.W. be transitioned into her
> mother's care), and he emailed her and called her a
> "ghetto bitch." The text messages and the email
> were not introduced at trail, and not made a part
> of the appellate record.
> While the court deemed the messages to be
> threatening to the extent that the court put a no con-
> tact order in place between Mr. Wise and Therapist
> W, and ordered Mr. Wise to anger management, it

is interesting that Mr. Wise's anger management therapist, T.B., testified that after completing therapy with Mr. Wise, and seeing the e-mail, he believed the email was "over the top," but not threatening. The court pressed him on it, and B continued to give his reasoning from a therapeutic standpoint, stating that after working with Mr. Wise, it was clear he did a lot of "emotional reasoning" when belittled, which resulted in him verbally defending himself. B stated that he, as a reasonable therapist, would not have felt threatened by the e-mail, even though the email was inappropriate. B tried to explain that he assessed Mr. Wise, and the results of that assessment, the court interrupted B, and said, "I make credibility determinations."

B went on to testify that he saw Mr. Wise twice a week for at least three months, that Mr. Wise successfully completed anger management, had shown vast improvement in his thinking, and had demonstrated that he was able to refrain from having knee-jerk verbal reactions to situations like he would in the past. While B was concerned that he did not know about the text messages or that Mr. Wise had interpersonal conflicts with DHS staff, B said that he sent an email to the caseworker when he began therapy with Mr. Wise, and asked for all information relevant to the issues Mr. Wise needed to work on, and nothing else was disclosed by the Department. B maintained that Mr. Wise was a fit parent "based on the logical reasoning he used in counseling" despite the court and the Department questioning him in depth about incidents regarding the manner in which Mr. Wise handled himself verbally with staff during the case.

Likewise, with Dr. DeYoub, Mr. Wise was not given any psychological diagnoses after his psychological evaluation, and Dr. DeYoub concluded that he was "capable of caring for M.W. should the court decide on a placement with [him]." The Department tried to persuade him to also change his recommendation by sending him the text messages and email to Therapist W, and "other documents related to [Mr. Wise's] behavior in another case, and while Dr. DeYoub stated in a responsive letter that the information was significant from a therapeutic standpoint and would suggest that Mr. Wise might have difficulty working with professionals for M.W.'s best interest, he still "may not have ruled him out as a possible custodian" even if he was aware of the information at the time of the evaluation. Dr. DeYoub said he would have suggested counseling and "maybe even anger management," which, of course, Mr. Wise successfully completed after these incidents climaxed between December 2012 and February 2013.

Despite Mr. Wise successfully participating in anger management, and demonstrating in the final permanency planning hearing on May 14, 2013, in which the court noted that Mr. Wise's "in -court behavior shows improvement," that he had benefitted from therapy, the court changed the goal of

termination of parental rights for M.W. Even though the court told Mr. Wise to remain in therapy (and he did), the court was convinced that for Mr. Wise, this was about winning the custody battle, and not about M.W. The court did not view Mr. Wise as being the non-custodial Father jockeying for recognition as M.W.'s father, but a man who had issues with women.

On June 21, 2013, the Department filed a Petition for Termination of Parental Rights and a hearing was set on August 6, 2013. It is from that hearing that this appeal follows.

OK, this is me talking again, Marcos Wise. Can you believe this? And they wondered why I had an "attitude" with these people. My appellant attorney was the first person that recognized my pain. I am internally grateful for her. What's so crazy is that if a male has any constructive criticism dealing with a female than they automatically put you in the category of hating women. Total B.S..

The other case in which they referred to was dealing with my Son J.W. that was taking place at the same time as this one. Remember the case I mentioned at the beginning of this book. My frustration climaxed. While no doubt I was over the top sometimes, these people behavior and including the Judge was inexcusable. He would rather satisfy a few worthless women than to do what was right for a little girl. How in God's earth was I suppose to have a good attitude about that?

One of the reasons I wigged out with Department of Human Services was because they were attempting a trial visit with the Mother. Back in the words of my appellant attorney footnotes: and I quote,

> "Perhaps Mr. Wise had incredible foresight, because M.W. was ultimately transitioned into her mother's home for a trial visit, and it ended disastrously after the mother was arrested on a multitude of child endangerment charges after she dragged M.W. across a Kroger parking lot by her ankles while leaving her two younger children unattended in the car."

The reason I am using direct quotes from L.L. my appellant attorney is because she allowed me to exhale in that someone saw this for what it was and was on my side. She then quoted after the above,

> "The other documents related to [Mr. Wise's] behavior in another case "to which Dr. DeYoub referred in his letter are included with the appellant record. The other case regarded a custody dispute over a son from another relationship, and the documents were filed during the same two months (December 2012 to February 2013) in which Mr. Wise's frustration level had climaxed in M.W.'s dependency/neglected hearing case. While Mr. Wise's behavior was no doubt "over the top" with that court as well, it is clear that Mr. Wise had, at that point, become the quintessential non-custodial father who felt bloodied by the court system. His behavior did not further his cause, but after viewing his situation with his children from his perspective (or through his "lenses," as Mr. Wise's anger management therapist put it), it is clear that Mr. Wise is not an unfit parent, but one who was being disregarded at every turn."

Once again this woman, and I am stating this WOMAN, because no one was able to relate and understand my plight more than she. How the do I hate all women when I admire this one and many more? I love my children so much and always have. No Court to satisfy their quota or to perpetuate this myth will ever stop that. I told these people to stop and let me love my baby the way I always have but they ignored that major aspect of her life which almost resulted in her demise. In my opinion they viewed my Daughter as one of their "cash cows" in that she generated revenue for the foster homes.

I want to continue to quote my appellant attorney L.L. from her argument on page 19, paragraph 2, of the Appellant Brief in the Arkansas Court of Appeals. And here we go:

"However, as previously discussed, While Mr. Wise readily and wholly admits that he was many of the things the court accused him of being, his anger and hostility did not surface until months into the case. Months of disregard by the court and the Department provoked him into becoming a wary, distrustful, and self-protective parent who could not make progress in obtaining custody of his child despite having no responsibility for her placement into foster care, and having completed every requirement with favorable results asked of him by the Department. Even after completing anger-management – a service intended to get to the root of his hostility, the court would not reconcile with Mr. Wise. This was despite the service having the intended effect of helping Mr. Wise see that his emotional reactions (reactions that many parents in his position would have had in this situation)

were not productive. Mr. Wise tried to reconcile his differences with the court by acknowledging that he was naïve at the beginning of the case and thought he would automatically be given custody of his daughter, and when that did not happen, he became defensive.

In fact, however, Mr. Wise was not naïve at all. He was legally due his daughter, and his reactions were justified in that the trial court's actions violated Mr. Wise's rights from the time M.W. was removed from her mother and placed in DHS custody. As noted by Justice Karen Baker in the Arkansas Supreme Court case of *Mahone v. Arkansas Dep't of Human Servs.*, 2011 Ark. 370, 383 S.W.3d 854, the United States Supreme Court has stated that it is a fundamental right to parent a child without interference by the state. 2011 Ark.370 at *6-7, 383 S.W.3d at 857-858 (citing *Troxel v. Granville*, 530 U.S. 57, 120 S.Ct. 2054, 147 L.Ed2d 49 (2000)). As she outlined in her partial dissent, before the state may intervene there must be a showing of unfitness on part of the parent. Without a specific showing of unfitness, there is a legal presumption that actions of a parent are in the best interest of the child. *Id.* Further, individualized assessment of each parent is necessary to prevent the arbitrary and unjustified interference with a parent's fundamental right to raise their child as they see fit. *Id.* (citing *Stanley v. Illinois*, 405 U.S. 645, 92 S.Ct. 1208, 31 L.Ed.2d 551 (1972)). One parent's actions should not negate the constitutional rights of the other. *Id.*

Yet here, just as in *Mahone*, the child was re-moved from the mother, and the non-custodial fa-ther was presumed <u>unfit</u> until he jumped through hoops to prove his fitness. Just as in *Mahone*, Mr. Wise did not enjoy a legal presumption of fitness. Just as in *Mahone*, Mr. Wise was not responsible for his child's removal by the Department, and yet re-unification with Mr. Wise was not the court's goal. Indeed, in explaining the course of action it took in this case, it stated that while Mr. Wise was enjoying expanded visitation and requesting custody, "we were working with the Mom," and [n]ormally, in these kinds of cases, we normally try to return the children to the parent from whom the children were removed. That's our order of priority; but, if that parent is taking too long, we ain't got no prob-lem looking at another viable parent if there's one out there. That statement is completely contrary to *Mahone*, which was reversed by our Supreme Court, as well as the Permanency Planning statute that was subsequently changed by our Legislature because of *Mahone*, which held that the primary goal of any case should be to return the child to <u>a</u> parent from whom custody was removed. *See Ma-hone*, 2011 Ark.370 at *4-5, 383 S.W.3d at 856-57.

At no time was Mr. Wise found unfit until the court and the Department continued to deprive him of the custody of his daughter, and pushed him to become verbally aggressive and angry months into the case. He deserved to have M.W. placed in his custody upon her removal, and if circumstances then developed such that M.W. was in danger with her father, the Department could have taken appropriate action based on those circumstances. Indeed, the goal could have continued to be reunification with M.W.'s mother even while her father enjoyed placement of her. See *Nance v. Arkansas Dep't of Human Servs.*, 316 Ark. 43, 873 S.W.2d 812 (1994).

Clearly, Mr. Wise should have been given custody of his daughter at the outset of the case. However, the error should not be compounded by the additional error of faulting Mr. Wise for his reaction to being deprived of custody for months, which landed him in anger management, for which the court then refused to give him credit. Essentially, the error in the legal proceedings provoked his anger, which was then used against him to label him as unstable and ultimately unfit. However, there was no evidence that Mr. Wise was unfit under either of the grounds cited by the trial court. Mr. Wise did not need services, but he completed every service the court required of him, and to the extent that he benefited from them, and issues the court believed rendered Mr. Wise unfit were remedied.

This was my Attorney's **CONCLUSION** to the Appellant Court:

"Clear and convincing evidence, as that standard is defined by this Court, was not met in this case, making the court's findings clearly erroneous. Although there are fragments of the evidence that

> support the trial court's findings, the evidence as a whole demonstrates firmly and definitely that the trial court made a mistake. *See Hopkins v. Arkansas Dept. of Human Servs.*, 79 Ark. App. 1,4, 83 S.W.3d 418, 421 (2002). Therefore, Mr. Wise prays this Court will reverse the trial court's decision and re-instate his parental rights."

My psychological exam expressed no diagnosis on me. And on cross examination the 25 year forensic psychologist still maintained that. The attorneys for the Department of Human Services stated that because I had a Masters Degree in Counseling, then I must have meandered or manipulated the tests. My home inspection was perfect. As a matter of fact two other independents also agreed with the Department's Psychologist.

It's funny that they felt I was unfit but in March 2013 an Arkansas Republican Representative by the name of Justin Harris adopted two little girls from this same institution. The girls were sisters and in foster care because of sexual abuse which left the two girls traumatized. The Harris's had three other biological sons in the home and soon handed the two young girls off to Eric and Stacey Francis, basically abandoning them. This is known in Arkansas as Rehoming. Soon after the older of the two girls were raped by Eric Francis in January 2014. He confessed to the rape and currently serves a 40 year sentence. There is no specific law against this practice currently while I write this book. I make that point to say this; "FOR REAL!" And me calling a few workers ghetto bitches was worse than that? This guy can adopt children but I can't have my Daughter? Oh and here is the Kicker; During the period that they were "Rehomed" this Representative continued to received State Funds from Arkansas for the care of these precious little ones.

This scenario also bought me to the conclusion that once a child is born a mouth suave for DNA should be conducted immediately, rather the couple is married or not. This can be done just as a newborn is checked for diseases and other medical conditions. This should be mandatory and part of the law. It makes sense not only from a moral and ethical standpoint but makes sense for fiscal responsibility. Let us start with the first reason:

1) If this is a federal mandate than there is no reason that the woman in the relationship can use the argument of miss trust, etc. It's the "law". And if something is in place that is a mandate than the misdiagnosing of paternity is bought to a minimal. If a paternity test is eminent from birth than potential lies and mistakes are cut off at the beginning instead of a lie gaining power and momentum. Which is no good in any aspect except for the individual creating the lie? And let's be realistic, the only being that is ultimately damaged from these massive untruths are the Children themselves. Imagine the pain and dysfunction that would be illuminated by this act? The only type of individuals that find a mandate of this type distressful are the women that use this manipulation consistently or the males that directly and indirectly participate in the facade.

2) Stopping Court hearings on useless information that could have been established from the beginning. Every year millions upon millions of dollars are spent for Court hearings and time after the fact in order to first establish Paternity. Why would you not think that this potential mandate would not make sense? I remind you this is Court Room time that could be spent on other issues such as keeping our society safer.

3) The overall safety of the Child's and/or young Adults' Health. Let's say hypothetically that this Child needs an organ or blood transplant from a parent. With these mandates in place it would stop these type of issues destroying a family at the finest level. That is the worst horrible time to realize a male is not the biological father? Imagine that for a moment? Not only do you have to contend with the failing health of your loved one but finding out at that time that your loved one is not biologically yours. Can you imagine the detrimental effects that would cause ultimately? And these are some of the situations in which males had to learn that they are not the paternal prodigy, How can "you", (the average person), and so am I, not see that this should be mandatory testing in our system of government and laws in the United States. (Mandatory DNA Testing and Swabbing for Paternity),? Especially before any male assumes and accepts responsibility for Paternity and Fatherhood. It's not just right for common sense, but correct most of all for morality and truth. Its funny that I have ran across so many people that claim that they are real but if you introduce something to them with Black and White Objectively, they will behave as if there is something wrong with you or the idea you proposed. At least some of the time through my lenses (mindset). So why not make it happen. And with this sentence I am not only speaking directly to my representatives of Arkansas, but the Federal government Judicial Body as a whole. Once again I feel this should be mandated whether the couple is married or unmarried. Georgia is a state that allows DNA testing for both married and unmarried couples at any time. They are ahead of the curve, which was a surprise to me. Usually liberal States are more susceptible to these types of mandates first. Kudos to you Georgia.

By knowing both parents, a child gains a greater sense of identity and belonging which is conducive for longevity.

My Daughter's mother was asked in Court at the beginning of this situation, does she Object to M residing with her Father during this situation and can you believe that she objected? This woman wanted to take a selfish-insecurity to the point of ignoring an immediate out for at least one of the children. Even with this surmountable life event, she could not release the bullshit. Do you understand me a little better now? Can you make sense of that? But we are superficially taught from little boys to respect a person solely based off of them possessing female organs. There is so much more than being a "WOMAN".

Now I want to touch on the question on why certain women participate in this type of behavior. For the most part I feel that it is a cycle of insecurity that is generational. But there is a more depressing issue that kept tugging at me. I thought about this possible reason in detail and this was the best logical conclusion (hypothesis) that I could muster. Here we go.

In every plight of a group of people is always an unspoken factor. The "elephant in the room" so to speak." Here is one concerning race equality concerning my people. Until we treat each other better and more fairly, it doesn't matter how many injustices are done against us because ultimately we are destroying each other more directly and indirectly than anyone or anything else. Until we deal with that issue no amount of police shootings and other wrongs will make a difference. I never hear Black leaders speak on this. The most important factor. As a matter of fact Good Mothers and people that don't carry those manipulative mindsets of the people in this book should despise their behavior just as much as I do because they make you (us) look bad also, rather you want to admit it or not.

Let us for a moment journey into the scope of racism. In today's racism it's not what it was of yester years but more of a systemic process.

I could care less about a group of people feeling a way towards me because of the hue of my skin. But what's bothersome is when that racism is carried out through calculated and methodical means. So let us explore that briefly. In today's society people can no longer use blatant slurs and tactics of racism, but instead have to depend on circumventing laws and using narrow minded people to assist them in those endeavors. One of which is Child Support Enforcement. Just like when Blacks were literally slaves the white masters still relied on other blacks to enforce their ideology and dominion. Without the help from those other blacks then that system would be less effective. We use the slang then and now describing those types of blacks as "House Niggers" or "Uncle Toms." So let's see who those types are today. What better way is it to bring down a Black Man than indirectly using the Black Woman. Every time a Black woman runs to a Child Support Office they put all of their business in the hands of individuals that has no ultimate care for their well-being. It is a business like anything else, the same way slavery was. Free labor and power. Are you following me? What is so funny is that the Custodial Mother does not receive the full amount of the Child Support payment. Child Support Enforcement takes out for fees and other processing costs. And at the front of the line doing this dirty work most of the time is the Black Woman; "Performing the Duties of the Master." While some women think that this is cute and have some satisfaction that they are getting back at a man, the institution that governs this activity has no ultimate respect for them and in actuality view them as no more than a modern day "Chicken George" from roots. And a lot of these Black women are falling for this tactic hook, line, and sinker. Meanwhile your viewed as merely a tool to help destroy your own race.

Going back to the Prelude of this book I want you to really think about how many times people have lied on you and it set you back so far. What was so sad about the matter is that it seemed that no one cared about the truth even for a second in your situation. Now imagine if you were on that end dealing with it as a Parent; and with the judicial system and basic society being negative toward you because of some lying women. Even having your family look at you in a negative light because these were "women" putting on an act. Throughout my Journeys in the last decade I have learned that there is a plethora of Black Men that want to be in their children lives but can't because of the manipulative tactics used by the Black Woman Custodial Parents. Not all of them but an overwhelming percentage that is disturbing.

Please do not think that I have a vendetta against Black Women. I have respect for all Women and People in General; Black, White, Hispanic and so on. But I despise a Fool; not being able to realize that a Stable and Loving Father is beautiful for their Kids. They rather keep up foolishness instead of realizing that because their in feelings about things that doesn't even matter. Trying to manipulate the situation and a Judicial System that allows it because its the Norm. Well "some" Judicial Systems. Enough is enough! When will this cycle be broken?

The Child Support and Visitation system is in dyer need of an overhaul. Just as in Healthcare Reform. The current Child Support system is outdated and consistently disenfranchises the non-custodial parent; Usually the Father. How is it that we can say that we care about our children when 50% of whom the children are is ignored as viable caretakers? If we are to move forward with being a better Black America than that is a fundamental understanding that "we" must adopt.

I came to this overall mindset by mostly my own personal experiences but keeping an open mind when speaking with other individuals and reading reports. How is it when you see something so plainly but try to convince yourself that its not there. That is the ultimate definition of insanity to me. When the objective brain observes something wrong but the emotional side of our brain tries to rationalize it. I can't ignore my objective mind anymore.

I am not naïve to think that there are no derelict non-custodial Fathers out there. But I just don't see it as much as it is portrayed in our society. Nearly at all. As a matter-of-fact I observed none. I am not bias toward Women of Color but I realized that (some) are just wrong to the core. I want to emphasize "some"as a nominal percent and not all. How wrong am I for having this mindset? Or am I wrong? As a matter of fact one of the most sexy, and intellectual woman in this world to me is Whoopi Goldberg because of many factors. I also highly respect the first lady Michelle Obama. I actually respect her more or just as much as President Obama because without her there would be no he. This couple showed not only the world but our community the way Black people should govern themselves. It is "ULTIMATELY" no more excuses in our community. I understand immediate issues out of your control. If we are to truly see ourselves equal, then we must realize that involves self-respect, unselfishness, and most of all self accountability. I have observed certain individuals B.S. themselves for many decades with no letting up in site. What is so funny about this is that these are the individuals that enjoy stating how "real" they are. Their definition of "Real" is to make sure people say what sounds good temporarily and at no means offer any constructive information that is accurate in that makes it inconvenient for their frame of thinking. In other words tell me what I want to hear and cater to my convoluted and hypocritical thinking.

I want the world to know that there are many fair and positive thinking Custodial Black Mothers in the world. I know this. But the focus of this book are those that are not. And how can you possibly love your child when you say "the hell" with their Father. Because of some issues that will never matter and most of the time self-imposed.

And let's not mention the incarceration rate for Black children, especially males without the guidance and love from their Biological Fathers. I use the term children in this statement also meaning grown children (Adults). Doesn't matter because their still our children.

There are great step parents but the potential influence of the actual Biological parent is immeasurable. The right of natural parents of their child is the pinnacle of natural rights. According to the website NAACP.org/ with their criminal justice fact sheet, "Blacks now constitute nearly a million of the total 2.3 million people incarcerated population. African-Americans are incarcerated at nearly six times the rate of whites." I remind you again that we only represent between 12 – 15 percent of the population. In my opinion you can see a correlation between our custodial parents having Child Support Enforcement/Elimination of Visitation as a default mindset and incarcerated Black males. Do you really think that the mainstream establishment respects us for that?

Regardless of these past perils I am making sure that I keep myself in a grounded situation for when my Children become adults. I want to be able to assist them not only financially, but spiritually and emotionally as well. I plan on being there for them always if they need me; No matter what! Raising a child does not stop at age eighteen. If I missed some time with them as Children than I will make up for it when their adults, which is just as important.

To all the Fathers that are out there feeling that they are alone and at times feeling isolated because of these unnecessary obstacles, please know that you are not alone. Please know that you are not crazy, a bad person, or all of the negative connotations society tries to superficially label you. Please know that sometimes the best you can do is to make sure that you are in a position to assist your children in the future if and when the need arises. Please know that I along with many other people understand your woes and plight. Keep your head up and mind healthy. Everything eventually comes out in the wash. And most of all stay out of prison.

With my kids still under age 18 this story is unfinished.

Marcos R. Wise holds a B.S. from Tuskegee University, located at Tuskegee, Alabama, in Animal Science (1997); and an M.A. from the University of Arkansas at Little Rock in Adult Rehabilitation Counseling (2013), Little Rock, Arkansas.

I would like to thank Ms. Leah Landford, Attorney at Law, Arkansas Public Defender Commission. She is a consummate professional that writes and communicate the greatest arguments for her clients. Once again thank you very much for your help from the bottom of my heart.